Elon Musk

Elon Musk's greatest lessons for business, life, entrepreneurship, and changing the world!

Table of Contents

Introduction 1

Chapter 1: The Dreamer 4

Chapter 2: Into Space, On The Road 10

Chapter 3: The Comeback 20

Chapter 4: The Future 24

Conclusion 31

Introduction

Embellished with the color purple due to the pervasiveness of the Jacaranda Tree, the city of Pretoria in South Africa is a marvel. Just north of Johannesburg, amongst the city's many notable features is its place as one of the prominent commercial and business hubs in the country. This is perhaps fitting for a budding entrepreneur, of which Pretoria has many. On June 28, 1971 one such entrepreneur-to-be was born in Pretoria, and his influence would go on to extend far beyond the Rainbow Nation.

The name Elon Musk is so well-known today, it could easily be on par with any everyday word used in the English language. When one sees him, one outwardly sees a passionate and ambitious entrepreneur who does not rest on his laurels. Despite achieving so much success, Elon Musk strives for more; at times, his ideas seem so out of this world (no pun intended!) that skeptics are quick to criticize him. But love him or hate him, Elon Musk cannot be ignored. And regardless of the opinion on his ideas for the future, one cannot help but admire his curiosity. Though he has come a long way from his childhood in Pretoria, listening to him speak evokes an image of the young curious child who dreamt of taking on the world.

His motivation behind his life's work has always had one primary focus: the betterment of humanity. For a boy who spent much time by himself, buried in his books, his concern for all of humanity matches that of many activists. While he is an ambitious businessman, he is not possessed by profits and the desire to become the world's richest man. In spite of the financial success he has achieved, he measures his own success by how his ventures improve the lives of his fellow human beings. With the Internet, he created one of the web's first online city guides. He followed this up with taking on the finance industry and introducing digital payments that have now become mainstream. Energy and space exploration are next on his agenda, and his ideas seem extraordinary. But for anyone familiar with Elon Musk's resume, his endeavors may be unusual but are always sure to make an impression on the world at large.

What goes on in the mind of Elon Musk is a mystery. The only conclusion one can draw is that his ideas seem absurd to many, and his harshest skeptics aim to denounce him. However, Elon Musk is like a stubborn child – unable to take no for an answer, preferring to prove his skeptics wrong. His career has been unusual amongst entrepreneurs and despite the ups and downs, he remains a significant cultural and business icon of the 21st Century, and will remain in the zeitgeist for decades to come.

Like all great stories about fascinating individuals, Elon Musk's story does not begin with splendor. It is through perseverance that he has been able to achieve the heights that he has achieved. His beginnings are no different from yours or mine, and his circumstances may not be considered ideal for someone who would later become one of the world's most prominent entrepreneurs. But for someone with aspirations to travel to Mars, no circumstance is ideal or not ideal; it is not the circumstance that matters, but the imagination – and Elon Musk has not lost the imagination he was born with. In fact, it has only continued to flourish.

Profit and adding numbers to one's bank account seems to be the prevalent goal of most business persons today. With this mentality, it is refreshing to see Elon Musk – who, despite becoming extremely wealthy from his ventures, is relentless in achieving his goals. He forgoes early retirement and a relaxed lifestyle in hopes of bettering the quality of life for all of humanity through his business ventures.

His story should serve as an inspiration to us all. Whether you are a budding entrepreneur or possess even the slightest interest in his endeavors, his sense of wonder has impacted our collective consciousness. His name is a "trending topic" in today's media. While that may seem trivial, what with everything else that clouds our news stories – it is without a doubt that Elon Musk's name will continue to trigger images of success, entrepreneurship, hard work, and inquisitiveness.

One of his Musk's companies is named after another great entrepreneur, Nikola Tesla. Perhaps in the future, another dreamer will name their company after a young boy from Pretoria who dreamt the impossible.

Chapter 1: The Dreamer

In this chapter, you will learn about the early days of Elon Musk and his eventual move to the United States.

South Africa

While the winner of the 1969 Miss South Africa competition was Linda Collett, one of the finalists was Canadian Maye Haldeman. Maye had settled in South Africa with her family after her adventurous parents decided to travel to the country to roam the famous Kalahari Desert. It was during her high school years that she met Errol Musk, who would later become an engineer. Errol's professional interests and Maye's own sense of adventure would be passed on to their children. They married in 1970 and went on to have three children together. Their eldest child, Elon, was born in 1971 in the city of Pretoria, South Africa.

The curiosity that Elon Musk possesses was not developed gradually, but rather it was embedded into his DNA. In an interview, he once stated that while his parents raised him, his primary influence was from his books. A voracious reader, he was particularly impacted by Isaac Asimov's Foundations series. One aspect of the series which struck a chord with the young Elon was that the series featured an enterprising scientist who wanted to save the human civilization from a foreseen Dark Ages by relocating humans on distant planets to inhabit. Perhaps an absurd and outlandish idea, but nonetheless, this vision was imprinted in Elon's mind and remains with him today.

While one may reflect on Elon's childhood and be impressed that the precocious child kept his face buried in Asimov's writings, it did nothing to improve his popularity (or lack of it) amongst his peers. The studious child was often bullied and had no choice but to put up with the constant abuse. Now over six feet and an imposing figure, it is hard to believe that Elon was the smallest child in his class and was the target of many bullies due to this. A notable incident which Elon has recounted several times is when a group of bullies threw him down a flight of stairs and then proceeded to beat him mercilessly until he lost consciousness.

Sadly, the torment did not end once Elon returned home from school. Though Errol and Maye were high school sweethearts, the love did eventually fade. At the age of 10, Elon's parents divorced. Maye got full custody of the three children: sons Elon and Kimbal, and daughter Tosca. However, Elon felt that his father was lonely and decided to leave his mother and siblings to live with Errol. He would later regret this decision deeply.

While Elon Musk is reticent to provide details about his time with his father, he stirs with emotion at the mention of him. The duration with his father remains harrowing to Elon, and he shudders when discussing this period in his life. To this day, Elon has a turbulent relationship with his estranged father. He feels that his father did not support him in his endeavors and would often belittle his achievements. Being called an "idiot" by his father was a natural and frequent occurrence.

While the quest for knowledge is often admired by adults, children seem to remain unimpressed and quite put-off. Such was the case with Elon. The Afrikaner culture at the time was very aggressive and full of machismo. Elon's brother Kimbal recalls that South Africa was not a peaceful country at the time, and as a result, violence was prevalent. This affected the young Elon and must have terrified him, as he was shy, introverted, and bookish. Elon's reservation and introversion made it difficult to make friends. He was often by himself – and though he is surrounded by friends and family today, there is still a loner quality to him. While he never outwardly expressed it, he lived in fear and was only at peace when alone with his thoughts. He was more comfortable when buried deep in Foundations, or The Hitchhiker's Guide To The Galaxy.

1983 was a turbulent year in South Africa. Nelson Mandela was 19 years into his prison sentence, yet his influence to bring down Apartheid continued outside of the walls of the prison on Robben Island. Though the Prime Minister, P.W. Botha, relaxed the rules on inter-marriage and miscegenation between the races, Apartheid continue to remain rampant. Elon Musk turned

12 years old in 1983, and he was just a few years away from serving mandatory conscription in the South African Defense Force for at least two years. Conscription was established in 1967, only four years before Elon was born. This was something Maye feared for both Elon and Kimbal. The Musk family were disgusted by the Apartheid system and did not wish to serve in a defense force that would allow it to thrive. At the tender age of 12, Elon Musk realized he had to flee South Africa.

While these dark moments may still haunt Elon Musk, it has not given him a pessimistic view of humanity. Anyone who has been subjected to vicious bullying might become bitter and wish to retreat into themselves. It would be farfetched to expect a bullied child to be concerned for the betterment of humanity; yet, such is the case with Elon Musk.

Headed West

Elon Musk remained in South Africa until 1989. It was in this year that he graduated from Pretoria Boy's High School. Following his graduation, he seized the opportunity to leave the country. Owing to his Canadian mother, he was able to obtain Canadian citizenship and migrated to Canada just before turning 18. Moving to Canada would start a new phase in Elon Musk's life, and it was Canada where he would begin his new life, though it was Canada's neighbor which he was really looking forward to getting acquainted with.

Elon Musk has stated that as clichéd as it sounds, the United States of America really is a land of opportunity. Canada, it seemed, was his gateway to the US. After spending two years as a student at Queen's University, he transferred to the University of Pennsylvania to complete his studies. He received two bachelor's degrees in Physics and Economics. Upon completion of his undergraduate degrees, he moved to California to attend Stanford University for further studies.

Yet, Stanford University did not seem to appeal to a young Elon Musk. After only two days, he dropped out, forgoing his studies in Applied Physics and Materials Science. However, this did not prompt him to leave the small town of Palo Alto. In fact, it was here where Elon Musk would first make his name in the world of entrepreneurship.

It was the mid-1990s, and Elon Musk was a long way from his home in South Africa. Though the country was now free from the Apartheid government which caused Elon to flee, it was clear that his new home was in the United States. And although Palo Alto is a small town, it has earned a reputation as being one of the hubs for business and technology in the United States. It is perhaps this reputation which caused the young boy from Pretoria to feel at home.

World Wide Web

Joined by his younger brother Kimbal, Elon decided to combine his passion for technology with his passion for business and start a new venture. The World Wide Web had taken off and many entrepreneurs were exploring this new phenomenon as an avenue for generating new businesses. Unbeknownst to the public at the time, the twenty-something Elon Musk had prior business experience during his childhood, which would lay the foundation for future business success.

One of the most popular mobile games of recent times is Flappy Bird; however, in the early 1980s, Elon Musk developed a game called Blastar, which, though he states is not as sophisticated as a game today, it still is far superior to Flappy Bird. In 1980, the Commodore VIC-20 was introduced and the young Elon became obsessed with the computer as soon as he got his hands on one. Within days, he mastered the use of this computer and designed the video game Blastar, which he later sold to a computer magazine for $500. While this may seem unimpressive in today's context, it was a big feat for a young child from Pretoria. This small feat would prepare Elon for future business success. Since Blastar was a video game that took place in outer space as its setting, it would serve as a precursor for Elon's later business ventures – though perhaps even young Elon could not predict what was to come!

The Musk brothers were rebellious in nature and continue to remain so. During his undergraduate years, Elon began to wonder what would affect the future of humanity. Sustainable energy and space exploration were two of his ideas. The third was relatively new, but its eventual influence on humanity would be incredible: The Internet and the World Wide Web. Elon and Kimbal did not set out to reinvent the wheel, rather they wanted to see how they could use the Internet to provide an existing service to a wider audience.

By now, the Musk brothers had traveled significantly. From a city in South Africa, they traveled to Canada, and Elon had lived in both Philadelphia and Palo Alto. Exploring these new worlds must have brought them a sense of curiosity as to what these cities had to offer. There must have been periods when Elon would leaf through volumes of city guides to see what each new city contained. Of course, a city guide was not created simply for Elon Musk; these were necessities for all humans – and one aspect of business that is consistent through all of Elon Musk's enterprises is to benefit humanity. He saw the Internet as a medium for reaching out to all of humanity, and he was about to combine his newly found interest in the Internet with the necessity of city guides.

Twenty-four-year-old Elon and twenty-three-year-old Kimbal founded Global Link Information Network in 1995 along with Greg Kouri. Greg was a real-estate developer and investor whom the Musk brothers met through their parents. Seeing the keenness and drive in the brothers, Kouri provided them with an investment to fund their crazy idea. Global Link became a service for businesses to advertise their services through the web. Many companies were skeptical and did not give importance to Global Link; many companies did not think there was a need or benefit to have an online presence at all. However, there were a handful of companies that decided to give the Musk brothers a chance and began to employ Global Link's services.

After only a year of operations, Global Link received a $3 million investment from Mohr Davidow Ventures. After this investment, several changes were made to Global Link. The company was renamed Zip2 and it was going to change its direction.

Chapter Summary

• Elon Musk was born into less-than-idyllic conditions in South Africa.

• Despite the struggle, he was inquisitive and had a desire to better humanity.

• He began his first Internet venture post-university and was set to create history.

In the next chapter, you will learn about Elon's most notable business ventures.

Chapter 2: Into Space, On The Road

In this chapter you will learn about how Elon changed the landscape of Internet business, and how he got involved with Space Exploration, and electric cars.

Internet Entrepreneurs

It is the year 1998. As the new millennium approaches, the world at large is hooked on the Internet. Business persons recognize its value and are seeking avenues to participate in the growing phenomenon. Skeptics are kicking themselves for not leaping at an opportunity during the early days of the World Wide Web. But for brothers Elon and Kimbal Musk, their leap of faith in the Internet has taken them to heights they may have never imagined.

By 1998, Zip2 had grown into one of the Internet's foremost directories for newspapers and other media outlets to construct their own directories advertising their services. Three years prior, they were met with many skeptics. However, in 1998, their client portfolio boasted names such as the Hearst Corporation, and The New York Times. The company was profitable, though it was not without its competitors. CitySearch was also launched in 1995, and its growth matched that of rival Zip2. As opposed to prolonging the fierce duel, Elon decided the best move forward would be for Zip2 and CitySearch to merge. By now, both companies were considered tour de forces in the realm of Internet businesses. Though Zip2 was known to "power the press" this time, it was them who were at the center of attention for the major press outlets. A $300 million merge was proposed; Zip2 would become part of CitySearch and the latter name would become the name of the company. Elon was Zip2's Chief Technology Officer and anticipated with baited breath the eventual merge of the companies.

However, the excitement soon died down. Though he was eager for the merge to occur, Elon realized there was a stark difference in company culture between Zip2 and CitySearch. Although a difficult decision, Elon decided it was best to cancel the merger. The fervor that was created by the press began to fade away. Yet despite this setback, things were not bleak. As Elon would learn, one closed door would make way for another, even greater opportunity.

One of the earliest and most formidable giants of the computer industry was Compaq Computer Corporation. Seeing the potential in Zip2, Compaq approached the company for a takeover. This time everything seemed right. In 1999, Zip2 was sold to Compaq for $307 million. Elon walked away with $22 million. He was only twenty-seven-years-old.

Most individuals in their late twenties who acquire several millions of dollars go one of two routes: some adopt an ostentatious demeanor and begin showing off their newly-acquired wealth, while more discerning individuals may invest their money and prepare for a very early retirement. While Elon Musk certainly presented himself like a rich man, he was not boastful of his wealth, nor was early retirement a thought on his mind.

X.com

Without waiting for the new year and the new millennium, Elon Musk began his newest venture in the same year that he sold Zip2 to Compaq. With money in his bank account, it was also embedded in his mind that his next venture would take on the financial industry in an unprecedented manner. X.com was launched in November 1999 as one of the world's first online banks. While online banking and digital transactions are commonplace today, this was unheard of at the turn of the century. Naturally, it was met with skepticism – but by now, Elon was accustomed to skeptics, and they did not frighten him at all.

PayPal

With his own funding, additional support from Greg Kouri and a partnership with Barclays, X.com managed to secure over 200,000 members in a matter of months.

However, history, it seemed, was repeating itself: X.com was not the first company to explore digital finance, and another company was rising in ranks – creating stiff competition for Elon Musk. Confinity was started by entrepreneurs, Peter Thiel, Luke Nosek, Ken Howery, and Max Levchin. Confinity had existed in the digital finance space for some time and were launching a new product for receiving and sending money via the web. This new product was called PayPal, and it would eventually become one of the world's largest digital finance products.

This time, a merger worked. Elon decided the best way forward was for X.com to merge with Confinity. This happened in the year 2000, and Elon became one of the forces behind the growth of PayPal. Though Peter Thiel was seen as a better choice for CEO, Elon's involvement helped push the company forward.

The year 2000 was not just a year for business and financial success for Elon Musk. It was in this year when he married his college sweetheart, Justine Wilson. Their first son, Nevada Alexander Musk, sadly passed away after only 10 weeks due to Sudden Infant Death Syndrome. They later had five sons, a pair of twins in 2004, followed by a set of triplets in 2006.

The dawn of the new millennium was welcoming for Elon Musk. Barely in his thirties, he was now a known entity in the world of Internet businesses. In 2002, only two years after merging X.com with Confinity, the stellar product PayPal was sold to eBay for $1.5 billion. Elon Musk ended his twenties as a multimillionaire and began his thirties as a billionaire. This would not have been expected for a young child from South Africa, growing up during the horrors of Apartheid.

Elon Musk had a definite goal as a university student: to do work that would impact humanity for the better. The Internet, sustainable energy, and space exploration were the three facets which he felt needed to be ventured into. With Zip2 and PayPal, he had mastered web entrepreneurship, and in an age where Internet entrepreneurs are created every day, they all knowingly or unknowingly owe much of their success to a young man from Pretoria with an insatiable curiosity.

Mission To Mars

Elon moved on from the Internet, and it was now time to begin his next venture. The stories he read in Isaac Asimov's Foundations series as a child remained imprinted in his mind, and a vision to travel to distant worlds had not faded from his life's ambition.

Exploration to outer space was a domain held exclusively by NASA. Recalling his boyhood days of being buried in Foundations and working tirelessly through the night to create Blastar, Elon Musk wanted to see how he could collaborate with NASA for their future endeavors.

Hari Seldon is a Professor of Mathematics at the fictitious Streeling University in the Foundations series. According to the study of Psychohistory (a fictitious study created for the stories), Seldon estimates that the Galactic Empire he inhabits will cease to exist in the future. As a result, he concludes that the only solution to rescue the human race from extinction is to populate other planets.

Though Hari Seldon only exists within the pages of the Foundations series, he also exists firmly in Elon Musk's mind. Perhaps as a young child, Elon likened himself to Hari, and to an extent, still does. In a conversation with entrepreneur Sal Khan, Elon stated, "I was trying to figure out why we'd not sent any people to Mars…" It sounds absurd to many, but for Elon, it was an obvious question. He felt that after Apollo, going to Mars was the "obvious next step." After a friend asked him what his next step was after selling PayPal, Elon expressed his interest in space exploration. However, he did not think this dream would come true, as space exploration was under the domain of a government, not of a private company.

He perused the NASA website to see if there was any information about traveling to Mars. Much to his disappointment, the website showed no signs of NASA wishing to travel to the red planet. By now, Elon Musk had become both unpredictable and predictable. One never knew what his next step would be, but one knew that if he saw a problem, he would solve it. Musk felt that the future of humanity would only be secure if the species could inhabit other planets. Mars was the ideal choice, and the preliminary step would be to grow plants to see if life could be sustained. Of course, to send the seeds to Mars, Elon would have to purchase a rocket.

Elon Musk was born in South Africa and had lived in Canada and the United States. Now, his next destination was Russia. In 2001, he traveled to Russia to see if he could purchase a rocket. With him was Jim Cantrell, an aerospace expert, and Elon's friend from his university days, entrepreneur Adeo Ressi. While space exploration was not out of the ordinary, the very notion of repopulating another planet was considered insane at best. Elon has recalled Adeo showing him a plethora of videos of rockets exploding; yet Elon is not bitter about this. On the contrary, he recalls these memories fondly. By now, Elon Musk was used to being looked upon as crazy; it did not matter to him, he would continue to do his work and prove everyone wrong.

While Elon was able to book a few meetings at prominent companies in Russia, he was initially met with a mixture of both scrutiny and scorn. Though he had conquered the world of Internet entrepreneurship, Elon Musk was not a known name in the world of space exploration and he was not about to be welcomed so easily. Jim Cantrell recalls one moment when an engineer actually spat at him and Elon as he felt both men were fools and amateurs. Elon may have been an amateur, but he certainly was no fool. This initial disdain that was thrust upon him did not seem to affect him at all.

The initial trip to Russia was uneventful, though Elon was convinced he would succeed. In 2002, he planned a second trip to the country. Bringing along Mike Griffin, who formerly worked for the venture capital wing of the Central Intelligence Agency, would surely bring their meetings to fruition this time. Sadly, this trip was also unsuccessful. What made matters worse is that Elon got the sense that the Russian companies did not possess an iota of respect for him. Enraged, he decided enough was enough. He had put up with bullying in Pretoria, but he was now a successful entrepreneur and the bullying would not prevail.

Elon returned to the United States with not a single rocket in his possession. Yet, being the incorrigible entrepreneur that he is, he was determined to make his dreams come true without any outside assistance. On the trip back from Moscow, the team were cheerful despite the failure of the meetings. Elon was working furiously on his laptop – what he was doing was anyone's guess. Then, he watched his team member's faces drop, as he stated that in lieu of buying a rocket from the Russians or anyone else, he was going to build a rocket himself.

Prior to his escapades in Russia, Elon had acquainted himself with the foremost individuals involved in space exploration. He had invited himself to organizations such as the Mars Society to make his intentions known. It was during this period that he met Mike Griffin, who would be one of his right-hand men in his space exploration venture. After much deliberation, he realized that participating with others would not work – nor would seeking assistance with others. Zip2 had been sold; PayPal had also been sold. It was time for Elon Musk to start a new company.

Space Exploration Technologies Corporation, or SpaceX, was founded on May 6, 2002. The mission of the company was to introduce space travel and exploration to the mainstream, and to expand humanity's existence to other planets. Elon Musk hopes to send human beings to Mars in the 2020s. However, for now, the capabilities of SpaceX are being tested.

Six years after the founding of SpaceX, Elon and his team introduced the world to a new rocket. The Falcon 1 was a marvel and will continue to be remembered for its splendor. On March 24, 2006, the world witnessed its launch. Perched on Omelek Island, in the United States' territory of the Marshall Islands, this would be the first time a privately-funded rocket would be launched. A sense of anticipation and excitement was prevalent all over the world. Elon Musk must have felt elated, as he was witnessing his boyhood dream come true.

At 22:30 Greenwich Mean Time, the Falcon 1 rocket was launched. One can only imagine the excitement that must have spread throughout the SpaceX headquarters. The rocket seemed to be a mark of supreme craftsmanship. Perhaps not even the keenest engineers could have predicted the corroded nut that was a part of an otherwise pristinely-kept rocket. The nut caused a fire and in less than thirty-seconds into its launch, the Falcon 1 rocket veered off-course and landed in the Pacific Ocean, to be devoured by its depth.

Perhaps for the first time in his adult life, Elon Musk felt defeated. And what a humiliating defeat it was! The magnificent rocket which he boldly said he would have his team build themselves did not last even half-a-minute. The vastness of the Pacific Ocean would erase its meticulously-crafted components forever. Elon's team could only think of one thing: they needed a drink. Yet, the relentless Elon had another thing on his mind: when would Falcon 1 have a second attempt?

Despite the disappointment of the first launch, the attitude at the SpaceX headquarters was one of optimism. Early on in his career, Elon learned that business would have setbacks and that it was imperative to keep his team motivated at all times. The initial merger between Zip2 and CitySearch did not work out initially, but this led to a better option – selling the website to Compaq. Maybe he did not outwardly express it, but he must have seen the failure of the initial launch as a promise for better things to come.

Electric Cars

Meanwhile, two fellow engineers and entrepreneurs were working on an exciting venture which they felt would revolutionize the automobile industry. In 2003, before the first launch of the Falcon 1, there was a growing interest in developing electric cars. General Motors had been the first player in the market, after releasing their EV1 Model back in 1996. While an electric car in the 1990s may have seemed revolutionary and game-changing, it sadly did not catch the public's fancy. A few models were sold, but in 1999, only three years after the EV1's release, the cars were recalled and later destroyed. It seemed the story of electric cars had come to a tragic end.

However, a new chapter in the story of electric cars was being written. Its authors were two engineers and aspiring entrepreneurs, Martin Eberhard and Marc Tarpenning. They were spearheading a new initiative to manufacture electric cars and make them affordable to the average consumer. They wanted to incorporate a particular name for their company. Martin Eberhard was planning on using the AC Induction motor for the cars, and so it seemed fitting that the company be named after the man responsible for its invention, Serbian inventor Nikola Tesla, and so the company was named Tesla Motors.

Eventually, as Tesla Motors began to gather steam, Martin and Marc realized they would need additional muscle to help the company grow further. In finding investors, one name sprung to their minds. Being a space geek, Marc had attended a conference of the Mars Society and had brought Martin along. They saw an enthusiastic speaker who had spent two days studying at Stanford University, where the conference was being held. This person was a complete amateur in the field of space exploration, yet he gave ideas reminiscent of the character Hari Seldon in Isaac Asimov's Foundations books. Martin and Marc decided to speak to this remarkable and eccentric character; though neither of them would have imagined they would work with him in a few years' time.

Elon Musk joined Tesla Motors after receiving a call from Martin Eberhard. It did not take much convincing for Elon to get on board. He was deep into work on SpaceX, but that did not deter him from taking the additional responsibility of Tesla Motors. Tesla Motors aims for a sustainable future – as its cars are electric and do not need gasoline. This goal to work for a more sustainable future was one of Elon's goals as a university student. Tesla Motors was right up his alley.

Being Tesla Motors' largest shareholder, Elon Musk became its Chairman. Under his guidance, Tesla Motors launched their first car in 2008. The Tesla Roadster was their sports car and was deemed to reintroduce the public to electric cars and revolutionize and disrupt the automobile industry. But just as SpaceX had its hurdles, Tesla Motors had its road bumps.

2008 was a trying year for Elon Musk. Both SpaceX and Tesla Motors were under his control, and it seemed that things were spiraling. After the failure of Falcon 1, the SpaceX team was working tirelessly to prepare for its next launch. On the Tesla Motors side, the team was preparing for the launch of the Tesla Roadster and launching the Tesla Motors brand to the public. Perhaps more than ever, Elon was under immense scrutiny; and perhaps for the first time in his professional life, the skeptics were waiting hand-in-mouth for Elon Musk's ventures to fail. Of course, the rebellious Elon did not cower in fear at the hounding of his critics; he was all set to prove them wrong. His relentlessness, however, did come at a price.

Personal Injury

The endless nights at the Tesla Motors office and investing his capital into the company, as well as into SpaceX, meant that Elon was neglecting his wife and sons. It seemed that his mind was only focused on his companies. He was persistent in creating products that would benefit humanity; sadly, he seemed to have forgotten some of the most important humans in his life. His wife, Justine, could not deal with the frustration any longer. In June of 2008, Elon and Justine divorced.

Divorces are never easy, and the aftermath of the divorce between Elon and Justine had its tremors. Elon Musk was not an ordinary businessman. He was an entrepreneur in the public eye, on par with any revolutionary American entrepreneur. His being from South Africa and coming to the United States made him an immigrant success story. He was also seen as somewhat of an eccentric due to his ideas with SpaceX. Being in the public eye brought his ventures more attention, but this attention came with its consequences.

In the divorce agreement, Justine requested a large sum of money, as well as shares of SpaceX and Tesla Motors. While her demands seemed reasonable and minor compared to what the billionaire had in his assets, the situation was more complicated than it appeared to be. SpaceX and Tesla Motors were struggling financially, and Elon was putting much of his own personal funds into the companies. Things were not going well for Elon Musk, and for the first time, his friends saw him spiral into a depression. He continued to persist with his companies, but something was not right.

Chapter Summary

• Elon changed the finance industry and the Internet with his involvement in PayPal.

• SpaceX got off to a rocky start, with the Falcon 1 failing during its anticipated launch.

• His venture into electric cars seemed doomed to fail.

In the next chapter, you will learn about how Elon bounced back from his failures.

Chapter 3: The Comeback

In this chapter, you will learn how Elon overcame hardship and brought SpaceX and Tesla Motors back from the brink.

Silver Lining

The man who wanted to go to Mars and populate the roads with electric vehicles was not feeling his best. Elon Musk was in a frenzy. After the failure of the first launch of Falcon 1, the second and third launches also failed. The humiliation was getting to be too much. He was not prepared to give in, but the struggle of his business venture and the end of his marriage had brought him much grief. Bill Lee, one of Elon's closest friends, noticed the depression in his friend and wanted to cheer him up.

Elon was reluctant, but he obliged Bill's demands and the two men went out to a nightclub. Through his connections, Bill managed to find a spot for him and Elon in the VIP area of the nightclub. It was then when Elon Musk was introduced to Talulah Riley. Talulah was a successful English actress. Like Elon, she was thrust into the spotlight – though she herself was unfamiliar with the strapping South African and his achievements. While he was slightly reticent, he spoke to Talulah and showed her his ideas for both SpaceX and Tesla Motors. She was intrigued by his ideas, but she was also enamored by Elon himself. It seemed that Elon felt the same about the dazzling star.

The intrigue between the South African and the Englishwoman would slowly develop into love. It seemed unlikely; Elon Musk was a billionaire entrepreneur in his late thirties, newly divorced, with five children and dreams of making an impact on both the Earth and Mars. Talulah Riley was a newly successful actress barely in her twenties. The pair did not seem ideal, yet the enamor did turn into love, and this newfound love helped Elon Musk take center stage once again.

Fourth Launch

On September 28, 2008, the Falcon 1 was launched for a fourth time. Perhaps the public had expected another failure, as there had been three consecutive failures. Elon must have been extremely anxious. Yet, things were looking up in his personal life, as he now had Talulah Riley on his side. This newfound enthusiasm and joy must have carried over to SpaceX. The fourth launch of the Falcon 1 marked the first time a privately-funded rocket would successfully orbit the Earth. Elon Musk was back in business.

The excitement and fervor surrounding SpaceX had improved tremendously. However, Elon still had one more challenge: he now had to ensure that Tesla Motors would also win over the public. The Tesla Roadster was not an immediate success. A popular website dedicated to automobiles entitled Truth About Cars was amongst Tesla Motors' harshest critics. They created a portion on their website viciously titled "Tesla Death Watch" to count down to when Tesla Motors would fail. The British television show Top Gear tested a Tesla Roadster which appeared to run out of power before it was expected to do so. The Tesla Death Watch and the Top Gear episode vehemently hurt Tesla Motors' image.

Elon did not take to these criticisms well. He was being hounded from all corners. His messy divorce had become newsworthy; all eyes were on Tesla Motors, yet these eyes were awaiting its downfall. SpaceX had met success with its fourth launch, but its second and third launches had received much scrutiny. This entire period was difficult for Elon, and his loved ones witnessed his rage. We may all presume that a billionaire does not have any financial woes, but this was far from true for Elon Musk. He was spending millions of dollars per month to keep his companies alive. He even began to ponder whether he should save SpaceX or Tesla Motors – his financial situation was that dire. He was borrowing money from his friends to keep the companies alive. He had conquered the Internet, yet it seemed that outer space was out of reach, and that the road would not welcome his presence.

Yet with the mounting pressure, Elon did not buckle down. He was determined to make things work. The success of Falcon 1's fourth launch gave him a sense of optimism, and he had to ensure that Tesla met the same success. His relationship with Talulah Riley had blossomed and in 2010 they married. Without a doubt, finding new love in his life was the silver lining in Elon's cloud. He was now more determined than ever to bring SpaceX and Tesla Motors to the forefront.

Model S

The Tesla Roadster was a luxury car, which despite immense criticism was slowly gaining traction. Many celebrities had purchased the Tesla Roadster. However, Tesla Motors still had to capture the mainstream eye – and to do this, they had to ensure their next model would appeal to a wider audience, outside of the rich and elite celebrities. The Model S was launched on June 22, 2012. As a sedan, this model would serve a more practical purpose than the Roadster and would appeal to a wider audience. It was a well-crafted revenge on his critics, as Elon Musk must have felt immense glee as he witnessed the success of the Model S. In its first year, the Model S became the highest selling electric car in all countries where it was sold. This feat continued in 2015 and 2016, and in 2017, it was second only to the Nissan Leaf.

The Model S silenced the critics, and with its warm reception, Elon made it known that like SpaceX, Tesla Motors was here to stay. Things were certainly looking up for Elon. While operations at SpaceX and Tesla Motors continued to thrive, there was yet another venture that was quietly brewing in the background.

SolarCity

The entrepreneurship genes must have been hereditary, as Elon is not the only forward-thinking entrepreneur in his family. One day, Elon was having a conversation with his cousins, Peter and Lyndon Rive. Impressing upon them the desire to create a more sustainable future to benefit humanity, Elon told them about the importance of solar energy and how he felt that this was another territory to be embarked upon. Little did he know that his cousins would take his words to heart and launch a business to implement solar energy throughout the United States.

SolarCity was founded by Lyndon and Peter in 2006. Within three years, the company began providing solar panels to residences and businesses throughout the country. Today, it is the United States' number-one provider of solar power. The Rive brothers asked their cousin Elon Musk to join SolarCity as the company's Chairman. In 2016, a decade after its founding, SolarCity was purchased by Elon and made into a subsidiary of Tesla Motors. According to a blog post written by Elon entitled The Secret Tesla Motors Master Plan (just between you and me), the ultimate goal of Tesla Motors was to move toward a "solar electric economy." Elon wrote that he believed this would ensure a sustainable future. This blog post was written in 2006, when SolarCity was founded and in 2016, by acquiring SolarCity, Elon was once again showing his determination to help humanity through a business venture. To a spectator, Elon Musk's life must have seemed beyond exciting. Yet, unbeknownst to the public, things were soon going to become boring!

Chapter Summary

• Elon felt a sense of joy after falling in love with actress Talulah Riley.

• The fourth launch of Falcon 1 brought SpaceX back to the forefront of space exploration.

• The Model S silenced Tesla Motors' critics once and for all.

In the next chapter, you will learn about the possibilities for Elon's future.

Chapter 4: The Future

In this chapter, you will learn about Elon's future endeavors, including a few tunnels he plans on digging!

The Boring Company

Elon Musk seemed to be on top of the world. He had become a crowned King of the Internet with his creation of Zip2, and later with his involvement in PayPal. Now, he was unstoppable with SpaceX and Tesla Motors. He had revolutionized the space exploration and automobile industries in an unprecedented manner. If one were to dismiss or criticize Elon Musk as the King of Transportation, they would soon eat their words.

The days of train travel within the United States seemed to have faded away. In simpler times, the railroads were flooded with the country's inhabitants looking to explore another mile or two of the vast landscape that comprised the nation. However, now, the primary purpose of trains within the United States is to carry cargo. Train travel for Americans is at an all-time low, a stark contrast to train travel in many other nations.

The city of Los Angeles is famous for many things and infamous for many other things. Amongst the city's less-attractive attributes is the traffic congestion. Elon, a resident of Los Angeles, had been stuck in the unforgiving Los Angeles traffic on several occasions. In a series of tweets, he vented his annoyance to his millions of followers. Half-jokingly, he tweeted about building a tunnel boring machine to so he could avoid the traffic. However, Elon Musk is not much of a joker and this apparent jest was to serve as the foundation for his next venture.

With SpaceX, Elon is determined to transport humans through outer space. With Tesla Motors, he is determined to alter the way humans travel on roads. With the Loop and the Hyperloop, he is determined to transport humans through underground tunnels. This new and exciting venture falls under the banner of Elon's company: The Boring Company.

The Boring Company aims to build transportation systems which will transport pedestrians, cyclists, and even cars from one part of a city to another, and even from city to city. To the skeptic's eye, this is another absurd idea by Elon Musk. However, when Elon announced his plans for the Loop and Hyperloop, the majority of the public were all ears. He had bounced back from the failures of SpaceX and Tesla Motors – and had shown the world that he was America's most interesting and daring entrepreneur.

In both Los Angeles where Elon lives, and Baltimore, plans to dig and build tunnels for the Loop and Hyperloop have begun. Elon is pushing for the completion to be rapid, and who knows? It is quite possible that you may be reading this book while sitting in a Loop or Hyperloop!

Artificial Intelligence

While Elon's goal has always been to use technology for the betterment of humanity, there is a growing concern that technology is doing a great harm to human beings. We are flooded with stories of a dystopian future; numerous studies are published on how we are addicted to our phones and to social media. One recent phenomenon which has caused much excitement is the advent of Artificial Intelligence or A.I. A.I. is not without its critics, and interestingly, one of its biggest critics is the prominent technology buff who revolutionized the Internet, transportation, and sustainable energy.

Elon worries that if A.I. gains too much power, it has the ability to take over humanity and cause us more harm than good. His friend, Larry Page, one of the founders of Google, is an advocate for A.I., yet Elon maintains his reticence on A.I. Elon's mission has been for technology to improve our lives, and he fears that A.I. will allow robots to gain dominance over humanity. A frightening thought indeed, and Elon insists that such will be our fate if A.I. is given too much power.

Getting Personal

Elon's personal life has not been without its rocky points. He has always been so buried in his own curiosity of the world that managing his relationship with his fellow humans is a challenge for him. He now enjoys a civil relationship with his ex-wife, Justine, and has split custody of his five children. He had a challenging relationship with Talulah Riley – they divorced in 2012. Talulah witnessed Elon during one of his most grueling times in his career. She aimed to be the light that would guide him to success, and indeed, he eventually found success with SpaceX and Tesla Motors. However, there was much pain left in him. A year after divorcing, Elon and Talulah reconciled and remarried, though this second attempt was short-lived, as they divorced again in 2016. Later in 2016, Elon began a relationship with the American actress Amber Heard. Sadly, this relationship also ended quickly – with the couple parting ways after only a year.

Elon's remains estranged from his father, Errol Musk. While the latter claims to be behind much of Elon's success, Elon denies much of this and states that his father brought a lot of sadness to his life and to his family's life. Much of his intellectual curiosity and sharp-mindedness is due to his inheritance from his engineer father, but Elon insists that this is overshadowed by the harm caused by Errol. Elon and Justine have forbidden their children from meeting their grandfather.

However, the relationship which Elon has with his mother, siblings, and cousins remains strong. Starting with Zip2, Kimbal Musk became an investor in PayPal and continues to be an investor in Tesla Motors. After inspiring his cousins Lyndon and Peter, Elon chairs their company SolarCity. When possible, he ensures he spends time with his mother, Maye, and sister, Tosca. When with his children, he shows them the world – recalling a time when they were in the company of the Prince and Princess of Monaco.

The Mystique

Elon Musk is a world unto himself. His vision for his business ventures do seem to have a control over his personality. His zeal has carried into his management style, and at times this has been to the chagrin of his colleagues and employees. While many individuals have stated their pleasure in working for Elon, many others have lamented about his firmness and intensity. Those who have lamented have either remained on board due to their passion for Elon's projects, or have left with a bitter taste in their mouth. He possesses a superior intelligence and viewpoint which many of us cannot even begin to fathom. As a result, he will not dumb himself down; one must catch up to Elon Musk. Despite these drawbacks, Elon continues to be revered. His supporters may liken him to a revolutionary and iconic businessman like Steve Jobs, yet Elon Musk is in a class by himself. Elon is certainly going to be remembered as a revolutionary. Though he has amassed billions, it is his ideas that spark our interest. In a time when an entrepreneurs' net worth seems to be the criteria for demanding respect, Elon Musk demands our respect for his many unique and life-changing ideas.

Achievements

Since the beginning of his journey into the world of entrepreneurship, Elon Musk has achieved in a few decades what many individuals would not achieve in their lifetime. With his relentless nature, many of the achievements you read may be overshadowed by even greater achievements. Here are some of the developments since his beginnings as an entrepreneur:

Zip2 is no longer in service. The site was purchased by Compaq Computer Corporation, which years later was purchased by Hewlett-Packard. The money earned by Elon from Zip2 was used for his next project X.com, which would later merge with Confinity to develop PayPal.

Elon Musk was eventually removed as CEO of PayPal. Peter Thiel was given this responsibility. However, as one analyzes Elon's professional career, he remains noted as one of the founders of PayPal. PayPal remains a billion-dollar company since being acquired by eBay. eBay has noted that in 2020, PayPal will not be at the forefront of their payment gateway. The company, though prominent, has been met with many competitors, such as Stripe. It has been targeted with much criticism and the future of PayPal is uncertain. A noteworthy event occurred when Elon repurchased X.com from PayPal. He stated this was for sentimental reasons, and later forwarded X.com to The Boring Company's website.

SpaceX has not stopped since the first successful launch of the Falcon 1. The Falcon 9 has achieved many milestones. SpaceX has been noted as the first privately-funded company to launch a spacecraft which successfully reached the International Space Station; this is one of its many achievements, and there are sure for more to come. Space exploration was once the exclusive domain of the government, but SpaceX has dispelled that notion and has given NASA and its foreign counterparts a run for their money. The ultimate goal remains to explore Mars. Elon has even stated that his goal is to die on Mars, once he knows that he will be leaving SpaceX in good hands.

Throughout the world, roads are becoming more and more occupied with electric vehicles. Amongst the different brands of electric cars, Tesla Motors stands apart from its competition. After making it the umbrella under which Elon's sustainable energy venture SolarCity would be run, Elon rebranded the company as Tesla, Inc. Continuing to provide electric cars for the common consumer, the Model X was launched in 2015. This SUV had over twice the amount of pre-orders as the Model S. In 2017, a new sedan called the Model 3 was released and has become immensely popular. For the future, another Tesla car is expected: The Model Y is slated for release in 2019 or 2020. Two additional models are the Tesla Semi and a new model of the Tesla Roadster. For a company that was expected to die, with many detractors wishing its death – Tesla cars seem to be going one place only – on the road.

SolarCity continues to dominate the solar power industry in the United States. From being a niche idea, it has found its way into the mainstream. The subsidiary of Tesla, Inc. provides solar panels for both residential and commercial properties. It continues to be run by brothers Lyndon and Peter Rive, and chaired by Elon Musk. Being an influence on his cousins since their childhood, Elon continues to guide the company in the direction for a more sustainable future.

The Boring Company is working feverishly to introduce a Hyperloop in the United States in the near future. Elon Musk continues to negotiate deals with state and city governments in hopes to build Hyperloop tunnels in a variety of cities. If his goals are met, it will revolutionize local travel and minimize daily commutes.

With his concern about the dangers of Artificial Intelligence, Elon started OpenAI with Sam Altman. This venture aims to research A.I. to ensure that once A.I. becomes more prevalent it does not harm humanity. It aims to find methods to develop A.I. in a manner that will be responsible and unthreatening to human beings.

Continuing with A.I., Elon developed Neuralink to improve conditions in the human brain through the use of Artificial Intelligence. The hope is that A.I. will also be able to treat diseases in the brain.

Elon Musk certainly has a lot on his plate and it would not be surprising if he piled more on! He continues to work non-stop to improve the human condition in any manner he feels he can. Elon looks at the achievements of the past to improve upon the conditions that may arise in the future. His attainments are almost unbelievable, and as we anticipate his next steps, we perhaps may not realize that in decades to come, we will look back on the heyday of Elon Musk and regard him as a giant who wanted to change the world – and did.

Chapter Summary

- Elon Musk has achieved success in three different areas of business – all for the betterment of humanity.

- His future ventures promise that even better things lie ahead.

- His achievements continue to amaze the world and will continue to do so for years to come.

Conclusion

South Africa has come a long way since the abolition of the Apartheid government in 1994. The nation is much more prosperous and, as a democracy, offers promise not offered before. As the nation is part of the BRICS group of nations, it is a rising global superpower. Among its many cities lies Pretoria, a bustling metropolis north of Johannesburg. While Pretoria is laden with the beauty of its Jacaranda Trees, its highlight remains its business district. Walking the streets of Pretoria makes one feel that they are walking in a city that breeds titans of the business world. With this in mind, it is no surprise that a boy born in Pretoria would become one of the world's most influential entrepreneurs.

The young boy would not have an easy journey. He was born in a country facing turmoil. It was looked upon with scorn due to its systematic racism. It was a country full of aggression and violence and was an unnerving environment for a shy and inquisitive child. However, this young boy never let go of his dream – to change the world and to better the human condition. He dreamt of traveling to the United States, the land of opportunity. He would learn about the various areas of the business world, and how he could impact humanity by being involved in these areas. Little did he know that he would enter all of these areas – and conquer them.

Elon Musk is an enigma, and even though his story is public knowledge, it seems to evoke fantasy matching that of any prominent novelist. Confident as he has always been, one wonders if Elon himself could have predicted his own success. Perhaps achieving success and becoming a rich businessman was not the main priority of a youthful Elon Musk. Though he has become a billionaire and a success story by any definition, his ultimate goal is more noble and outlandish than any of his contemporaries.

While his business ventures are varied, there has always been one agenda behind them: to better the experience of humankind. While Elon has been candid about many of his life experiences, it remains a mystery as to what caused him to develop this concern for the future and betterment of humankind. As a child, Elon grew up in a cruel atmosphere. His native country ran a system called Apartheid which kept the White Afrikaners in a position of privilege and viciously oppressed Black, Colored, and Indian South Africans. As if this atmosphere was not enough, Elon witnessed the cruelty of his father and was subject to his malice during the years he lived with him. At school, his intelligence and inquisitiveness did not save him from the constant bullying he was put through. With all this cruelty, Elon Musk must have wanted a better life not only for himself, but for all of humanity. He wanted to ensure that behind all his future business ventures, the ultimate goal of a company would be to serve humankind.

With Zip2 and PayPal, his goal was to use the new phenomenon of the Internet to serve as a platform for people to conduct business. Zip2 helped businesses advertise their services and use the Internet to reach a wider audience. While this is commonplace and a requirement for any business today, this was unheard of in the 1990s, and the view that the Internet is an area to promote one's business to the world is partly thanks to the innovation of Elon Musk. With PayPal, Elon raised eyebrows by utilizing the Internet as a space to conduct financial transactions. Once again, this was absurd in the early 2000s, but because of Elon's endeavors, an entire industry called "e-commerce" exists and continues to flourish.

SpaceX and Tesla Motors are two marvels of which only Elon Musk could be the mastermind. While humanity has become comfortable with the idea of space exploration, the idea of venturing past the moon has not been looked into. That is, until an amateur came along to shake things up. Inspired by the fictitious Hari Seldon, Elon feels confident that SpaceX will slowly but surely help humanity survive by populating on Mars. With Tesla Motors, Elon ensures that humanity will have a more sustainable future by switching to electric cars.

With SolarCity, Elon plans to continue working toward a more sustainable future. By installing solar panels, it hopes to use the Earth's natural resources to generate power. A simple idea from Elon inspired his cousins to start the business and have him join to lead the path. Now under the Tesla Motors company, the future for this solar-focused energy venture certainly looks bright.

One is puzzled when looking at Elon Musk's resume. His experience is so varied that one cannot tell what he will do next. "Anything" would be the only appropriate answer. His goals were to use the Internet, outer space, and sustainable energy to better the lives of his fellow humans. While there is still much that he wishes to achieve, in less than half-a-century, he has managed to make an impact on all three fields. As a young university student, he set these goals in mind, and despite the ups and downs, his vision has remained clear and his persistence has been unbreakable. What the future holds for Elon Musk is anyone's guess.

But one thing is certain: it will be spectacular.

www.ingramcontent.com/pod-product-compliance
Lightning Source LLC
LaVergne TN
LVHW021050100526
838202LV00082B/5420